teach me about

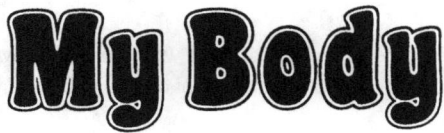

Copyright © Joy Berry, 2022
Originally Published, 1986

All rights are reserved.

No part of this book can be duplicated or used without the prior written permission of the copyright owner, except for the use of brief quotations from the book.

For inquiries or permission requests contact the publisher.

Published by Joy Berry Enterprises
www.joyberryenterprises.com

teach me about

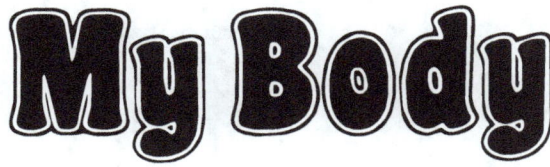
My Body

By JOY BERRY

Illustrated by Bartholomew

I have a body.

My body has many wonderful parts.

My **head** is a part of my body.

I have **hair** on the top of my head.

I have hair on the back of my head.

I also have hair on both sides of my head.

I have two **ears**.

There is one ear

on each side of my head.

I have a **face**

on the front of my head.

There is a **forehead**

on my face.

There are two **cheeks**

on my face.

There is also a **chin**

on my face.

I have two **eyes** on my face.

There are two **eyebrows** above my eyes.

There are **eyelids** that cover my eyes.

There are **eyelashes** on my eyelids.

I have a **nose** on my face.

I also have a **mouth** on my face.

There are two **lips** on my mouth.

There are **teeth** in my mouth.

There is also a **tongue** in my mouth.

I have a **neck** that attaches my head to the rest of my body.

I have a **chest** on the front of my body.

There are two **nipples** on my chest.

I have a **belly** on the front of my body.

There is a **belly button** in the middle of my belly.

I have a **back.**

I have a **waist**

in the middle of my body.

I also have two **hips.**

I have two **shoulders**.

There is an **arm**

attached to each shoulder.

There is an **elbow**

in the middle of each arm.

There is also a **wrist**

on each arm.

I have a **hand**

at the end of each arm.

There are five **fingers**

on each hand.

One of my fingers

is called a **thumb**.

There is a **fingernail**

on each finger.

I have two **legs**

attached to my body.

There is a **knee**

in the middle of each leg.

Above each knee is a **thigh**.

Below each knee is a **calf**.

Below each calf is an **ankle**.

I have a **foot**

at the end of each leg.

There are five **toes**

on each foot.

There is a **toenail**

on each toe.

All of my parts

make a wonderful body that

can do many wonderful things.

helpful hints for parents about

Dear Parents:

The purpose of this book is
- to bring to children an awareness and appreciation of their bodies, and
- to teach children the appropriate names for the basic external parts of their bodies.

You can best implement the purpose of this book by
- reading it to your child, and
- reading the following *Helpful Hints* and using them whenever applicable.